W9-AOE-991

# 365 Days...
# with my
# faithful
# Dog

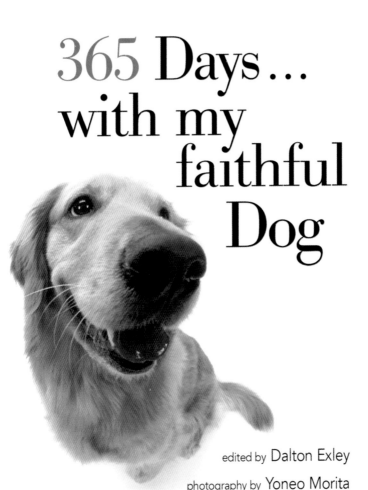

edited by Dalton Exley

photography by Yoneo Morita

MJF BOOKS | New York

Published by MJF Books
Fine Communications
589 Eighth Avenue, 6th Floor
New York, NY 10018

*365 Days with My Faithful Dog*
LC Control Number: 2018945253

ISBN 978-1-60671-428-7

Photography copyright © 2012 by Yoneo Morita/Hanadeka™
Selection and arrangement copyright © 2016
by Helen Exley Creative Ltd.

This edition is published by MJF Books in arrangement
with Exley Publications Ltd.

Printed in China.

MJF Books and the MJF colophon are trademarks
of Fine Creative Media, Inc.

[1010]   10   9   8   7   6   5   4   3   2   1

# The dog was created especially for children.

HENRY WARD BEECHER (1813–1887)

A dog's love is unconditional and its companionship unsurpassed.

ANNABEL GOLDSMITH

Dogs want and need what
we do: friends, sunshine,
play, and love.

JEFFREY MASSON, B. 1941

Dogs offer one of the most stable and enduring friendships on this earth.

WILLARD SCOTT

There is always one dog in your life that is the gatekeeper: the one who opens your heart to others.

PETER EGAN

The smallest of dogs can
fill a room with love and healing and
their very presence
in the home can eliminate
depression or sadness.

BILLY ROBERTS, FROM *THE HEALING PAW*

# He was a very bad boy yet with a heart as boundless as a summer sky.

JOHN GROGAN

A dog has one aim in life.
To bestow his heart.

J. R. ACKERLEY (1896–1967)

No matter where you are, your dog
will welcome you home.

BEL MOONEY

A dog wags its tail
with its heart.

MARTIN BUXBAUM

O ne can only slip down
so deep in one's thoughts when
a dog is around.

ROY MACGREGOR

Anyone who adopts a pet can learn
something about faith, hope,
and love.

CHRISTOPHER S. WREN

T here
is simply no
*down* to dog.

ROY MACGREGOR

They ask so little in return for what they give, yet they give so much, and they give in silence.

JOHN O'HURLEY

# Dogs don't do grumpy.

JENNI MURRAY

# Dogs want and need to be loved.

STEVEN WINN

A dog's only ambition is
to give you all his love.

STUART & LINDA MACFARLANE

They exude gratitude with every
windshield-wiper wag of their tails,
and clear away the
mists of our discontent.

MARI GAYATRI STEIN

Walking your dog is life affirming…it's as if you're plaited together, one extended consciousness, awareness overlapping.

BRUCE FOGLE

My dogs have taught me to
appreciate more fully and
assume much less.

JOHN O'HURLEY

All knowledge, the totality of all questions and answers, is contained in the dog.

FRANZ KAFKA (1883–1924)

There's something very touching about an animal that is dependent on you for everything.

PHILIP TREACY

She was joyous and beautiful and
a constant symbol of happiness.
Although she obviously emulated us,
sometimes I wonder.
Shouldn't I have emulated her?

BROOKS ATKINSON (1894–1984)

# Dogs can tell when they're around dog lovers.

MARK R. LEVIN

$W$ithout dogs the world would
seem a lonely place…

LOYD GROSSMAN, FROM *THE DOG'S TALE*

They recognize that we provide for them what they cannot provide for themselves. They love us for the kindness of that responsibility. We love them for the joy and affection that they return. It is a perfect, constantly renewing circle.

JOHN O'HURLEY

Dogs don't bear grudges.

SUE TOWNSEND

A dog: companion, friend,
protector, playmate and life-changer.
Dogs add a dimension to our lives
that otherwise would be just a vacant
spot. They work for us, guard us,
play with us, entertain us, love us,
keep us company,
and change
our lives.

H. NORMAN WRIGHT

Go into the park on your own and start talking to strangers, and people will think you are at best a sad, lonely git, and at worst a child molester. Go in with a dog and everybody talks to you.

ELINOR GOODMAN

Dogs are healers. They are
enlightened. They seem to have
figured out how to live beautifully
so much better than we humans have.
While we struggle to figure out why
we were put here on Earth, all a dog
wants is to love and
be loved —
a powerful lesson
for us all.

DR. BERNIE S. SIEGEL

A pup does not know words.
It just hears love.

PAMELA DUGDALE

I realized I hadn't experienced much love, joy, and exuberance in years. She brought with her zest for life and a playfulness that ignited a spark in me that I'd let fizzle without realizing it.

SAGE LEWIS

Our dogs…gave us the gifts of love,
protection and comfort in the
sad and tough time….Dogs
really are our very best friends.

WILLARD SCOTT

In dogs, we find true and faithful companions, who love you whether you are a vagrant living under a bridge or the richest person in the world.

RYAN O'MEARA

I've always believed that life is rubbish without a dog to come home to. No matter what kind of day you've had, they're always delighted to see you.

CAROLINE QUENTIN

As diverse as each of us are, a love
for dogs brings people together.

WILLARD SCOTT

It doesn't take much to make a dog happy: just the little things, the basic things. It is an important life lesson dogs teach us, and my dogs taught me.

MARK R. LEVIN

This enigmatic animal that
stumbled into my life…
gave me reason to pause, to slow
down, to relax, and to pay mind to
the fullness of my life.

SHANE GALLOWAY

Dogs belong to that elite group of con artists at the very pinnacle of their profession, the ones who pick our pockets clean and leave us smiling about it.

STEPHEN BUDIANSKY

Dogs, like children, become
emblems for who we are
out in the world.
We can't help letting it happen.

STEVEN WINN

Buy a pup and your money
will buy love unflinching.

RUDYARD KIPLING (1865–1936)

Dogs…bring us back to life, haul us into the present, make us get on with things instead of moping.

BEL MOONEY

# Dogs allow you to express your emotions in a very straightforward way.

JUDITH SUMMERS

He never sulks,
never mopes, never
shows me anything
other than
the deepest
affection.

RICK STEIN

What joy they have brought. What companions. In a frantic and demanding life, my dogs have been a sanctuary. Far from any judgment and expectation, they offer unconditional love — and I seem to mean as much to them as they mean to me.

JACKIE STEWART,
B. 1939

# What is it that cats, humans and dogs have in common?

Our devotion to love.

JEFFREY MASSON, B. 1941

Dogs seem to see into our souls and offer us kindness, devotion, and complete acceptance. We talk to them and sing to them and take them on rides in the car because we know they like the car.

MARY TIEGREEN

I truly believe God created dogs for a cause. They are the greatest companions a man could ever have.

MICKEY ROURKE

Don't make the mistake of treating
your dogs like humans, or they'll
treat you like dogs.

MARTHA SCOTT

It doesn't surprise me to discover that people who have a close and affectionate relationship with a dog suffer less stress, are less likely to suffer a heart attack and, if they do, are more likely to recover.

JENNI MURRAY

The dog is the only being that loves you more than you love yourself.

FRITZ VON UNRUH

Frankie and my other dogs have taught me that life is abundant in beauty and love.

BARBARA TECHEL

Dogs and cats are my passion. Their love is unchanging, unconditional, and unbounding in warm kisses and wiggling bodies.

GINGER ROGERS (1911–1995)

He is so shaggy. People are amazed when he gets up and they suddenly realize they have been talking to the wrong end.

ELIZABETH JONES

They have taught me to believe
in the constant goodness that seems
to emanate so easily from their
gentle and loving nature.

JOHN O'HURLEY

You can't fool a dog. Dogs know when you're sad. They sense when you need them.

ALLEN & LINDA ANDERSON

When you need to feel loved there is nothing quite like having a dog look up at you with adoring eyes.

NIGEL FARNDALE

My dog, she looks at me sometimes
with that look, and I think maybe
deep down inside she must know
exactly how I feel.
But then maybe she just wants the
food off my plate.

AUTHOR UNKNOWN

We give dogs time we can spare,
space we can spare, and love we can
spare. And in return, dogs
give us their all...

M. ACKLAM

# Dogs have got us exactly where they want us, and we, idiotic grins fixed to our faces, go along with it all.

STEPHEN BUDIANSKY

# The friendship and loyalty of dogs help human beings to get through just about any of life's changes and sudden curves.

ALLEN & LINDA ANDERSON

His gentle being calms and sustains me. The way he runs to me and presses into my body, or sits quivering on my feet at the least frightening sound, kindles in me the most satisfying protective instincts.

JAN FOOK

Pets rarely harm us at all. They love us without conditions, as a matter of course. Their love is of a pure and rare quality. For us, an indulgence. Perhaps an addiction. And when it's removed the hurt is extreme.

STEPHEN DOWNES

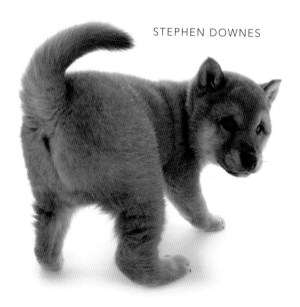

I loved him much more than
I thought anyone could love
an animal. I loved his silliness,
clumsiness, kisses and protectiveness.

DIANA M. AMADEO

When you tire of puppies…
you tire of life!

AUTHOR UNKNOWN

A relationship with a dog also helps us know ourselves better. A dog is guileless and utterly honest. It becomes a unique mirror reflecting us back to ourselves, if we pay attention.

BROTHER CHRISTOPHER

Dogs give us so much joy.

DEBRA BURLINGAME

A wise dog can teach us much of what we need to know. Patience. Caring. Companionship. And love.

PAM BROWN, B. 1928

# Dogs are good friends; their loyalty is unswerving.

ALLEN & LINDA ANDERSON

# My goal in life is to be as good a person as my dog already thinks I am.

AUTHOR UNKNOWN

It is hard to deny that we feel a very fundamental, innate, unlearned, and in that sense quite irrational attraction toward cute little things, especially helpless cute little things. Dogs take advantage of this no end. They play us like accordions.

STEPHEN BUDIANSKY

Maybe what I like about dogs so much is their appetite for life. They are so "up," so thrilled to see you.

MARTIN CLUNES

Every dog owner believes his dog
to be exceptionally intelligent
and charming…

THEODORE DALRYMPLE

# Good dogs win all the ribbons, it's true. But bad dogs have more fun.

JOHN GROGAN

There's something magical about a wet nose thrust into your hand as you settle down to watch TV, and a warm healthy body curled up at your feet.

EDWINA CURRIE, B. 1946

S andy…had more than enough
love for everyone.

TERESA AMBORD

He is your friend, your partner, your defender, your dog. You are his life, his love, his leader. He will be yours, faithful and true, to the last beat of his heart.

AUTHOR UNKNOWN

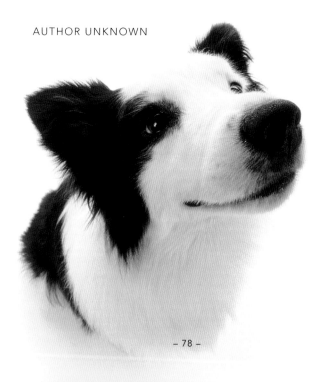

Dogs make us feel better.

JAN ETHERINGTON

# Whoever said
you can't buy happiness

forgot about puppies.

GENE HILL

Being with a dog, understanding her moods, her wants, her feelings, her emotions, without the need for words, returns you to the core of your being.

BRUCE FOGLE

Dogs have an enormous capacity for helping people forget their worries and anxieties.

ALLEN & LINDA ANDERSON

Dogs give us so much devotion and
loyalty in return for our care.

AUTHOR UNKNOWN

Every dog would have a home, and every home would have a dog.

AUTHOR UNKNOWN

A very small dog can fill a very great gap in one's life.

PAM BROWN, B. 1928

Dogs…teach us to stop thinking of ourselves; they take away our self-pretense and make us live in the moment. They are wonderful creatures, all of them.

PETER EGAN

Sometimes a dog comes along that really touches your life, and you can never forget her.

JOHN GROGAN

I think perhaps one of the greatest
reasons I love dogs so much is that
they, like me, refuse to act their
age and continue their "puppydom"
for their entire lives.

PETER EGAN

When you have a dog…in your life, you are truly blessed for that close kind of bond that you won't find anywhere else.

JAY WILLIAMS

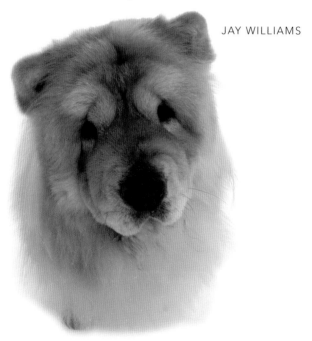

He behaved like he owned me, not the reverse, and I was his property in a sense.

PHILIP TREACY

My two little muppets are unbridled love and joy; I can hardly imagine they will one day be gone. That they love me so unconditionally is such a gift, one I sometimes feel unworthy of.

RORY FREEDMAN

# He is the little heartbeat at my feet.

CHARLES PATRICK DUGAN

He's very affectionate and he loves me so much, and it's always nice to be loved to that degree.

JUDITH SUMMERS

The beauty of having a dog,
even a very old dog,
is that the dog gets you out
no matter what the weather, no
matter what the mood.

ROY
MACGREGOR

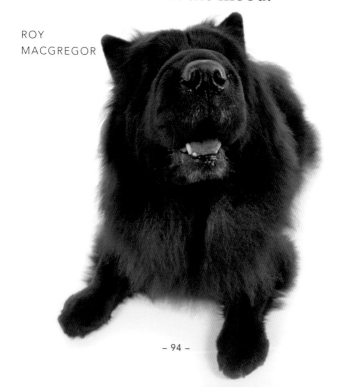

Goofy showed me that it is being able to give love that we crave. A dog rejoices in this communion: there is no cold shoulder; no shrinking from our touch.

BELINDA HARLEY

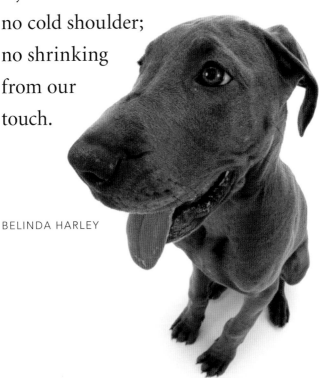

Medical studies have shown that people with regular access to dogs visit the doctor less often, have lower blood pressure levels, and suffer fewer incidents of heart disease and dementia. Pet companionship can even motivate seniors to increase daily activities and socializing.

STEVE DUNO

It is amazing how much love and laughter they bring into our lives. Dogs are one of the wonders of life and add so very much to ours. It's just the most amazing thing to love a dog, isn't it?

JOHN GROGAN

Dogs are born knowing exactly what they want to do: eat, scratch, roll in disgusting stuff, sniff and squabble with other dogs, roam, sleep, have sex. Little of this is what we want them to do, of course. We ask them to sit, stay, smell pleasant, practice abstinence, and be accommodating.

JON KATZ

Dogs teach us how to love with an open heart, and how to live in joy.

AUTHOR UNKNOWN

There is something in him that evokes the greatest tenderness from people. His mere presence seems to bring out the better aspects of human nature.

ANTHONY DANIELS

A man's best friend is his dog.

LORD BYRON (1788–1824)

To your dog, you are more than just a friend; you are the leader of the pack, his protector, his provider, and an all-knowing god.

STUART & LINDA MACFARLANE

Once a dog loves you, he loves you always, no matter what you do, no matter what happens, no matter how much time goes by.

JEFFREY MASSON, B. 1941

Dogs bring out the best
in humankind.

PAMELA DUGDALE

# Sign on bulletin board:

"Puppies for sale:
The only love that money can buy."

Rarely did he take his beautiful, kind eyes off me…and wherever I went there he would be too, and wherever I sat he would…sit beside me — close, protecting me, his head on my knee.

ELIZABETH VON ARNIM (1866–1941), FROM *ALL THE DOGS OF MY LIFE*

Dogs, no matter their breed, all have an inner beauty. They have kind, gentle hearts and a real need for company and affection.

STUART & LINDA MACFARLANE

Peple need a measure of happy simplicity — and a dog supplies it. Unqualified love — and very few demands.

CHARLOTTE GRAY, B. 1937

A life, a warmth, an intelligence.

A kind companion.

A dog.

PAM BROWN, B. 1928

Soft big eyes, gentle and quiet. She is patient and loving — just what any stressed-out human needs.

HELEN EXLEY

A dog believes you are what you think you are.

JANE SWAN, B. 1943

Every dog deserves a smile, a word of admiration, a little reassurance — especially if he is very ugly or very sad.

PAM BROWN, B. 1928

Dogs come in all shapes and sizes, yet every one, you must agree, make humans perfect company.

STUART & LINDA MACFARLANE

A dog knows that if he sits in front of you long enough and pleads with every look and wag — you'll eventually give in and take him for a walk.

PAM BROWN, B. 1928

Puppies look like very small
children whose mothers have bought
a size or two too big clothes.
To give them growing room.

MAYA V. PATEL, B. 1943

Adorable little puppy who will snuggle up to you, nibble your ear, gambol and romp all over the place…worming its way into your heart, making a slave of you…

BUSTER
LLOYD-JONES

What can we call them?!;
A huddle of pups? A wriggle of pups?
A squirm, a shove, a muddle of pups?
A drowse of pups? A sprawl of pups?
A totally out of this world of pups?
And all gathering the energy to
become a rush, a plunge,
a stampede of pups.

CLARA ORTEGA, B. 1955

Your little dog has never even seen a rabbit — but watch when he's asleep. He's chasing down a mammoth.

PAM BROWN, B. 1928

The smart dog quickly discovers that, to get what he wants, one mournful look is much more effective than a frenzy of barking.

STUART & LINDA MACFARLANE

A dog likes to sit under
the dining table.
Just in case.

PAM BROWN, B. 1928

We believe in ourselves because of
the trust our puppy has in us.

MARGOT THOMSON

He is your friend, your partner, your defender, your dog. You are his life, his love, his leader. He will be yours, faithful and true, to the last beat of his heart.

AUTHOR UNKNOWN

$\mathrm{O}$ld age means realizing you
will never own all the dogs
you wanted to.

JOE GORES

How strange to think Dog was
once simply Dog. For see how we
have squashed him and stretched
him. Yet inside every variation
is that first and utterly
basic Dog.

PAMELA DUGDALE

# Every dog is beautiful in its own way.

STUART & LINDA MACFARLANE

A dog will continue to trust when it has been betrayed.

CHARLOTTE GRAY, B. 1937

# Here's love.
## Disguised as a mop.

PETER GRAY, B. 1928

# If a dog's prayers were answered, bones would fall from the sky.

PROVERB

If he wanted a dog biscuit, he simply sat near the box of biscuits and silently stared at one or the other of us. If he not merely wanted a biscuit but felt it was positively his right to have one, the silent stare was accompanied by a lowering of the head.

GEORGE PITCHER, FROM
*THE DOGS WHO CAME TO STAY*

# The world would be a sadder place without puppies.

PAM BROWN, B. 1928

Just a scruffy little dog....And yet you are the best, the kindest friend anyone could have.

MARGOT THOMSON

Happy is the dog who has found a kind human — he will forever have someone to tickle his tummy.

STUART & LINDA MACFARLANE

'Tis sweet to hear the watch-dog's honest bark
Bay deep-mouth'd welcome as we draw near home;
'Tis sweet to know there is an eye will mark
Our coming, and look brighter when we come…

LORD BYRON (1788–1824)

Poor dog! he was faithful and kind,
    to be sure,
And he constantly loved me,
    although I was poor;
When the sour-looking folks sent me
    heartless away,
I had always a friend
    in my poor
    dog Tray.

THOMAS CAMPBELL
(1777–1844)

We simply loved them with all our hearts; we perhaps even loved them — I'm not ashamed to say it — beyond all reason. And they loved us, too, completely, no holds barred. Such love is perhaps the best thing life has to offer.

GEORGE PITCHER, FROM
*THE DOGS WHO
CAME TO STAY*

Dogs bring special gifts to the lives
of those who live with them.

ALLEN & LINDA ANDERSON

# A dog is love for a lifetime.

PAM BROWN, B. 1928

It is hard to imagine that these flubsy little scraps — all feet and tail and belly — will grow into disciplined and beautiful dogs. But they will.

PETER GRAY, B. 1928

No one appreciates the very special
genius of your conversation
as a dog does.

CHRISTOPHER MORLEY (1890–1957)

I realized, it was not I who was looking at the dogs, but the dogs who looked at me, and each dog with the same look in the eyes…the same hope, the same hopelessness. "Can I come with you? Can I be your dog? Can't I be your dog? No?"

ERIC PARKER, FROM *BEST OF DOGS*

A dog is a smile and a wagging tail.
What is in between doesn't
matter much.

CLARA ORTEGA, B. 1955

W hat a very small, what a very ordinary dog. No pedigree and very little looks — but a creature full of life and love.

PAMELA DUGDALE

"Some enchanted evening…"
And so it is with pups and people.
A seething mass of small, yapping,
prancing puppies — and one stands
out like a star. Your puppy.

PAM BROWN, B. 1928

P̲uppies are nature's remedy for feeling unloved…plus numerous other ailments of life.

RICHARD ALLAN PALM,
FROM *MARTHA, PRINCESS OF DIAMONDS*

# What are little puppies made of?

30% cuteness

29% mischief

28% affection

10% soft fur

3% innocence

STUART & LINDA MACFARLANE

Pug is come! — come to fill up the void left by false and narrow-hearted friends. I see already that he is without envy, hatred, or malice — that he will betray no secrets, and feel neither pain at my success nor pleasure in my chagrin.

GEORGE ELIOT [MARY ANN EVANS] (1819–1880)

A puppy can smell dinner through double glazing and heavy oaken doors and brick and concrete and a casserole dish.

PAMELA DUGDALE

Dog's Maxim
on Relaxation: The secret to being
completely relaxed is to have a human
to do all the worrying for you.

STUART & LINDA MACFARLANE

There is so much we can learn from Tuts. About loyalty and love. And a complete absence of selfishness. Tuts seems to exist to give us happiness. I know that when I'm stressed out, all I need to do is summon him for a back-scratch.

SHOBHA DÉ, FROM *SPEEDPOST*

# A dog trusts deeply and so is easily betrayed.

CHARLOTTE GRAY, B. 1937

"Won't be long" means nothing to a dog. All he knows is that you are GONE.

JANE SWAN, B. 1943

"Go in your basket," says Master in his sternest voice. And the puppy obeys. Enters the basket, tail down, turns round a time or two —

and then leaps out beaming from ear to ear and rushes over for a pat.

PAM BROWN,
B. 1928

Foss took this ancient responsibility very seriously. He used to chase aeroplanes, rushing out into the garden and barking at them till they flew away. Then he would come in again, breathing rather heavily, with an expression of satisfaction at a job well done.

CELIA HADDON, FROM *FAITHFUL TO THE END*

# Animals are such agreeable friends — they ask no questions, they pass no criticisms.

GEORGE ELIOT [MARY ANN EVANS] (1819–1880)

I am unable to imagine how
anybody who lives with an intelligent
and devoted dog can ever be lonely.

ELIZABETH VON ARNIM (1866–1941),
FROM *ALL THE DOGS OF MY LIFE*

"Oh! Please! Tell me how I get out of these amazing clothes. I've been struggling with them for hours and hours. I don't think they're me at all…or are they? I am sort of gorgeous, and look kinda cute, don't I?"

Fence in your garden, block all gaps with wood and wire. Spread the lawn with toys. And after a while the man next door will knock on your door — a jubilant puppy squirming in his arms.

PAM BROWN, B. 1928

The one absolutely unselfish friend that a man can have in this selfish world, the one that never deserts him, the one that never proves ungrateful or treacherous, is the dog.

SENATOR GEORGE GRAHAM VEST (1830–1904)

I felt a silent current of love from him — strong, steady and deep — unceasingly flowing to me....For someone who has never had this kind of experience with a pet, there are no words to adequately explain it.

SUSAN RACE

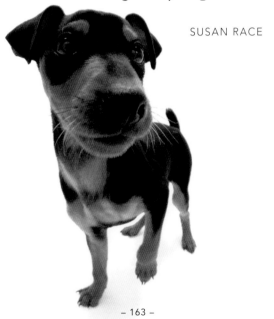

The reward of owning a well-behaved, loving and intelligent dog is beyond measure. Those who have owned such a dog are truly blessed.

BARBARA WOODHOUSE (1910–1988),
FROM "THE FAMILY PET"

This is the pup that will worry a glove to death. Kill a shoe. Rip a toilet roll to shreds — and run a mile if it sees a mouse.

PAM BROWN, B. 1928

$N$ot Carnegie, Vanderbilt, and Astor together could have raised money enough to buy a quarter of a share in my little Dog Snap.

ERNEST THOMPSON SETON (1860–1946)

Beauty without Vanity,
Strength without Insolence,
Courage without Ferocity,
and all the virtues of Man without
his Vices.

LORD BYRON (1788–1824),
FROM "EPITAPH TO A DOG"

A dull day, a sad day, a frustrating day — but everything seems bright when a small furry object hurls into your arms and tells you how very glad he is to see you home.

PAM BROWN, B. 1928

A dog will never break your heart, betray your trust, or abandon you when you are needy and afraid, in the throes of madness, or drowning in the lagoon of your emotions.

MARI GAYATRI STEIN,
FROM *UNLEASHING YOUR INNER DOG*

Dogs are always more delighted than anyone else in the family to see you return from work.

SALLY MORRIS

Dog, n. A kind of additional or
subsidiary Deity designed to catch
the overflow and surplus of the
world's worship.

AMBROSE BIERCE (1842–C. 1914)

To hold a living creature, to learn its loveliness, to feel its heart beat in our hands, to know its trust, is at last to understand that we are kin. Is to rejoice in life. Is to lose all loneliness.

PAM BROWN, B. 1928

Dogs have stolen our hearts, our homes and our wallets, not necessarily in that order.

AUTHOR UNKNOWN

A dog smiles with its whole face —
ears, eyes, nose, whiskers,
mouth, tongue.

PAM BROWN, B. 1928

He's a brilliant, ordinary,
incredible companion and
my little prince.

ROXANNE WILLEM SNOPEK

What jolly chaps they are! They are much superior to human beings as companions. They do not quarrel or argue with you. They never talk about themselves, but listen to you while you talk about yourself.

JEROME K. JEROME
(1859–1927)

Dogs, no matter their breed, all have an inner beauty. They have kind, gentle hearts and a real need for company and affection.

STUART & LINDA MACFARLANE

Give a pup a home and a little
love and he will give you
his heart forever.

PAM BROWN, B. 1928

One has to be very devoted to dogs
to endure the loving attention
of a slobberer.

CHARLOTTE GRAY, B. 1937

A happy dog, however young,
however small, holds its head high
— being loved, being wanted, being
your companion.

PAM BROWN, B. 1928

Never bite when a simple growl will do. Never growl when looking cute will do. No matter what you've done wrong, always try to make it look like the cat did it.

STUART & LINDA MACFARLANE

I believe by far the greatest number
are owned just for the sheer delight
of having a lovely creature round the
house to be admired, to admire you.

BARBARA WOODHOUSE (1910–1988)

Keesha was my friend,
my confidant, my angel
and, ultimately,
my teacher.

SUSAN CHERNAK
MCELROY, FROM
*ANIMALS AS
TEACHERS AND
HEALERS*

A melancholy face came round
the door — the feet edged forward.
And joyfully he came towards me —
inch by inch, foot by foot. His tail
exclaiming his affection.

PAM BROWN, B. 1928

Most dogs don't think they are human; they know they are.

JANE SWAN, B. 1943

There is a special bond created
between an animal and its owner,
one built on unconditional love.

LEO MCKINSTRY,
FROM *DAILY MAIL*, FEBRUARY 18, 2003

Rules for My Human:
Do not dig up my bones while
gardening. Keep to your own part
of the bed. Be attentive to my every
need. Take me for walks
every time I ask!

STUART & LINDA MACFARLANE

When all other friends desert, he remains. When riches take wings, and reputation falls to pieces, he is as constant in his love as the sun in its journey through the heavens.

SENATOR GEORGE GRAHAM VEST (1830–1904)

Your dog just doesn't notice that
you are old or ill or unsuccessful.
To him you are perfect.

PAM BROWN, B. 1928

However large the house
a puppy will always
be underfoot.

PAMELA DUGDALE

Humankind is drawn to dogs
because they are so like ourselves —
bumbling, affectionate, confused,
easily disappointed, grateful
for kindness.

PAM BROWN, B. 1928

A dog
appreciates the
person who knows all the right
places to scratch.

CHARLOTTE GRAY, B. 1937

If your dog
decides
it is time
for his
walk —
there's not
a great deal
you can do
about it.

PAMELA DUGDALE

I wag my tail and your blues fade away, I snuggle close and frown turns to smile, I play catch and your world fills with laughter. And all I ask in return, is two meals a day…and all your love.

STUART & LINDA MACFARLANE

One cute little puppy can turn
a king into a jester.

STUART & LINDA MACFARLANE

Dogs have a way of bringing you back to earth. Their affection shames pretense. They are guileless.

GARRISON KEILLOR, B. 1942

Dog's Maxim on Friendship:
Your very best friend is whoever
is holding the bone.

STUART & LINDA MACFARLANE

Tugs brought new meaning to the term "adoration." Wherever I went, he wanted to be there too. He never took his eyes off me and with a simple glance in his direction, his whole body wagged with happiness.

SUSAN RACE

A wise dog can teach us much of what we need to know. Patience. Kindness. Caring. Sharing. Companionship. And love.

PAM BROWN, B. 1928

Montmorency's ambition in life is to get in the way and be sworn at. If he can squirm in anywhere where he particularly is not wanted…he feels his day has not been wasted.

JEROME K. JEROME (1859–1927)

The love for a well-chosen dog can transcend life itself.

STANLEY COREN

Thousands of generations of dogs have, in their heart of hearts, believed that one day, if they listen hard enough, and concentrate, they will eventually master human speech.

MAYA V. PATEL, B. 1943

Even a puppy will endure the
unendurable out of love.

PAM BROWN, B. 1928

Your dog stands and quietly whines; it's time to drop your worries and take the little guy for a walk.

HELEN EXLEY

He is loyalty
itself. He has taught
me the meaning
of devotion. With him, I know
a secret comfort and a private peace.

GENE HILL

We must choose the strongest pup, the cleverest, the most active. So why do we choose the most helpless, tiny, tiny dog, all eyes and rumpled fur?

PAM BROWN, B. 1928

Whether I have been away for a working week or just two minutes across the road buying a bottle of milk from the village store, Buster always welcomes me home as if I am a hero returning from the wars.

ROY HATTERSLEY

# A dog can talk you into most things — silently.

PAM BROWN, B. 1928

And when we bury our face in our hands and wish we had never been born… he looks up at you with his big, true eyes, and says with them, "Well, you've always got me."

JEROME K. JEROME (1859–1927)

A pup is like a baby. It goes on trusting long after it has been betrayed.

PAM BROWN, B. 1928

Daisy, her name is…she was named that when I got her, on which day she immediately took over the management of my life.

DOROTHY PARKER (1893–1967)

How can any of us explain how we feel…in the early morning, when the animal we have chosen to share our lives is standing…waiting, to renew the pleasure of our presence.

JOYCE STRANGER

"He'll grow out of it"
has more hope than certainty.

PAM BROWN, B. 1928

Your little dog gulps down his food.
Before the hyenas and the
vultures arrive.

PAM BROWN, B. 1928

I, who had had my heart full for hours, took advantage of an early moment of solitude, to cry in it very bitterly. Suddenly a little hairy head thrust itself from behind my pillow into my face…drying the tears as they came.

ELIZABETH BARRETT BROWNING (1806–1861)

A cat does not betray the fact that he has done something diabolical. A dog is racked with guilt — and so gives the game away.

PETER GRAY, B. 1928

Java taught me how to be a better person by being an example of unconditional love and peace.

SAGE LEWIS

# Who needs words when your eyes and tail can speak for you?

PAM BROWN, B. 1928

His enthusiasm for each new day
was infectious.

KAREN WHEELER

There is no psychiatrist in the world like a puppy.

BERN WILLIAMS

I am going to be a guard dog.
Eventually. I think. But not yet.

PAM BROWN, B. 1928

Charley likes to get up early, and he likes me to get up early too. And why shouldn't he? Right after his breakfast he goes back to sleep.

JOHN STEINBECK (1902–1968)

All they ask for is the most basic shelter, food and water, and in return they give us unbounded, unflinching affection.

LEO MCKINSTRY, FROM *DAILY MAIL*, FEBRUARY 18, 2003

There always seems to be more skin
to a puppy than it can possibly need.

MAYA V. PATEL, B. 1943

# Sometimes doing absolutely nothing is quite enough for one day.

STUART & LINDA MACFARLANE

How sensible. He looks you in the eye and sees you as an equal. He is courteous and kind. A gentleman.

PAM BROWN, B. 1928

If you are patient with your human
he will soon learn a few dog words
such as dinner, fetch and walkies.

STUART & LINDA MACFARLANE

"Get away, Ugly, you beastly dog!"
he would say. And the dog would be
apparently in an ecstasy of enjoyment
at being called anything at all.

SIR JAMES WALPOLE

He is your friend, your partner, your defender, your dog. You are his life, his love, his leader. He will be yours, faithful and true, to the last beat of his heart.

AUTHOR UNKNOWN

If the doctor insists that you try exercise, acquire a puppy. He will take over the entire treatment.

JENNY DE VRIES

Many a day he pulled me away from my solitude, anger, laziness and greed.…He covered me with wet sappy kisses and warmed me with big howling welcomes.

ROMA IHNATOWYCZ

A well-trained dog will make no attempt to share your lunch. He will just make you feel so guilty that you cannot enjoy it.

HELEN THOMSON

My friend has a fine watch dog.
At any suspicious noise he wakes the
dog and the dog begins to bark.

LEOPOLD FECHTNER

There is invariably one dimwit in the litter — but what he lacks in sagacity he usually makes up for in bumbling charm.

CHARLOTTE GRAY, B. 1937

They invite us to be exuberant and playful without needing a reason.

MARI GAYATRI STEIN

Show a dog an ounce of love and he'll be your friend for life.

STUART & LINDA MACFARLANE

She has crawled into the deepest corners of my heart, the places that hold the most love — and the most pain.

CAROLINE KNAPP

Brave little fellow. He was only a little puppy when he took on the whole world to defend me. He was absurdly brave. And it was there and then that I determined to return his love and be all that he expected of me.

HELEN THOMSON

Even asleep, he will detect someone scraping out the last remnants of Marmite from the jar in the kitchen four floors below and thunder downstairs to lick it clean.

TREVOR GROVE

# When you come home your dog says, "You're home! I love you. I love you. I love you."

PAM BROWN, B. 1928

Oh, the saddest of sights
in a world of sin
Is a little lost pup with his
tail tucked in!

ARTHUR GUITERMAN

Heaven goes by favor. If it went by merit, you would stay out and your dog would go in!

MARK TWAIN (1835–1910)

# It is always disconcerting to carry on a conversation with a dog whose eyes are totally invisible.

PAM BROWN, B. 1928

Little puppies in pet shops should have a warning sign above their cages: "Do not look into my eyes, for I will kidnap your heart."

STUART & LINDA MACFARLANE

[Your dog] never knows that you have been mean or jealous or grasping. It encourages you to be kindly and when you respond, it loves you.

SIR JAMES WALPOLE

His head on my knee can heal my human hurts.

GENE HILL

W hen the world is at its dismal,
dullest, darkest, your dog will insist
on his walk — and cheer you
back to sanity.

PETER GRAY, B. 1928

The one absolutely unselfish friend that a man can have in this selfish world, the one that never deserts him, the one that never proves ungrateful or treacherous, is the dog.

SENATOR GEORGE GRAHAM VEST
(1830–1904)

There is nothing so guilty as a guilty dog.

PAM BROWN, B. 1928

I have found that when you are deeply troubled there are things you get from the silent devoted companionship of a dog that you can get from no other source.

DORIS DAY, B. 1922

No matter
how little
money and
how few
possessions you
own, having a dog
makes you rich.

LOUIS SABIN

"Beg!" I say. "Sit!" I say. "Down!" I say. And he smiles — and wanders off.

PAM BROWN, B. 1928

# CHOOSING A PUPPY

He looked clumsy, ugly, toothless, but utterly adorable, totally irresistible. He just had to be mine.

MARGOT THOMSON

The dog goes to sleep in his basket.
You wake up with him in the bed.

PETER GRAY, B. 1928

All right, so I don't know how to bury my garden messes. And I bark at everything. But I love you, love you, love you, and I will go on loving you till the day I die.

PAM BROWN, B. 1928

# You never forget a beloved dog.

MARK R. LEVIN

A dog desires affection more than its dinner. Well — almost.

PAM BROWN, B. 1928

Basil Harris qualifies for the Guinness Book of Wreckers; he has already eaten two Chesterfields (one leather and one synthetic) and three pairs of Charles Jourdan shoes.

JILLY COOPER, B. 1937

# If you have dogs, then you're never on your own.

ANTHEA TURNER, B. 1960

Dogs are great listeners. You can rattle on for hours about all your problems — they won't interrupt even once and will never, ever criticize.

STUART & LINDA MACFARLANE

# In its dreams the most domestic dog is wild and free.

PAM BROWN, B. 1928

The agility of his ears deserves a chapter to itself, their eloquence reflecting alertness, intent listening, relaxation, or eating mode, when the ears become horizontal like side-view mirrors.

VALERIE GROVE

Our dogs trust us. They don't question our intentions. They make us feel good about ourselves, and we are better people because of them.

MARI GAYATRI STEIN

The dog…never seems to change, not even when the end is there. Your coming through that front door remains, right to final tail wag, the single most significant event in the history of that moment — for the moment is all that they live for. And living for the moment is the secret that they give to us.

ROY MACGREGOR

There's something so floppy and droopy and heavy and drowsy — so wriggly and snuggly and nibbly about a pup that you wondered how you ever managed without him.

PAM BROWN, B. 1928

A dog friend just doesn't care who you are — fat or old or none too steady on your pins. Just so long as you love him.

CHARLOTTE GRAY, B. 1937

There was a clear division of duties in the house; Lucky would sit, looking out of the window, guarding the house — I would do everything else.

STUART & LINDA MACFARLANE

Dogs have their own unique, loving ways to let us know that in times of crisis, in times of celebration, in times of daily life, we are not alone. A wag of the tail, a lick, and a hug are some of the not too subtle ways that dogs express their love. Each day, a dog tells you, "I adore you!"

WILLARD SCOTT

The rich man's guardian and the
poor man's friend,
The only creature faithful to the end.

AUTHOR UNKNOWN

If friends fail us, if the phone is silent and the postman passes, our dog will touch our knee, and smile, and say, All the more time for us to be together. Come for a walk. This is a splendid day.

PAM BROWN,
B. 1928

No home is complete without a dog…or rather, no home is complete without a dog, a chewed carpet, a soiled bed, scratched furniture…

STUART & LINDA MACFARLANE

D̲ogs…once they love, they love
steadily, unchangingly,
till their last breath.

ELIZABETH VON ARNIM (1866–1941),
FROM *ALL THE DOGS OF MY LIFE*

One of the saddest sights is to see a
Dane ill. Their big eyes are a picture
of misery, for a sick Dane puts on
everything it can to get all the love
and sympathy.

BARBARA WOODHOUSE (1910–1988)

When a dog has sprawled in a place where someone is bound to tread on him, the extended paw and pitiful whimper can make the inevitable appear entirely your fault.

PAM BROWN, B. 1928

The bond between man and dog is something that is almost absurdly strong. We who experience it feel almost ashamed to admit it to those people who do not understand or share it.

ANTHONY DANIELS

There is no sadder sight than a reprimanded dog. With tail between his legs and head held low, he will scuffle away to a lonely solitude, waiting for your forgiveness.

STUART & LINDA MACFARLANE

A dog will sense when you are sad or anxious. With a cheery "Ruff, ruff," she will climb onto your lap to lick your face…

STUART & LINDA MACFARLANE

The Dog will not criticize you for all your human failings. He is always there when you come home, manifestly thrilled to see you even if you have only been out to empty the dustbin for thirty seconds.

VALERIE GROVE

# A dog wilts under the words "You bad, bad animal."

PETER GRAY, B. 1928

The games that delight dogs entail endless repetition. Stop throwing the stick and his eyes will reproach you. "Once more. Please."

PAM BROWN, B. 1928

No matter how badly we behave, or how low we feel, dogs are always there to greet us, full of loyalty and kindness.

LEO MCKINSTRY,
FROM *DAILY MAIL*, FEBRUARY 18, 2003

He will kiss the hand that has no food to offer, he will lick the wounds and sores that come in encounters with the roughness of the world. He guards the sleep of his pauper master as if he were a prince.

SENATOR GEORGE GRAHAM VEST (1830–1904)

A dog can add years to an old person's life — someone to care for, someone to come home to, someone to talk to. A dear friend.

PAM BROWN, B. 1928

Dogs know that life is too precious to go into battle over something trivial. But people do it all the time.

RYAN O'MEARA

It doesn't matter whether we are royalty or rogues; our dogs don't care. What we are doesn't matter. Who we are doesn't matter. Our dogs reward us with their loyalty…

JOYCE STRANGER

A dog is all heart. And stomach.

PAM BROWN, B. 1928

No one with good dogs is ever
truly alone.

JON KATZ

A quiet gentle dog will bring a quiet, deep satisfaction to your whole life.

HELEN EXLEY

So my good old pal, my irregular
dog, my flea-bitten, stub-tailed friend,
Has become a part of my very heart,
to be cherished till lifetime's end.

W. DAYTON WEDGEFARTH

His name is not Wild Dog any more, but the First Friend, because he will be our friend for always and always and always.

RUDYARD KIPLING (1865–1936)

We are simply
two life forms
journeying in
time in acceptance
and love for each
other's essence.
And what in life
is better than
that?

SANDRA LUND

It is always said that however many wonderful and happy years a dog lives, you know that one day, the day he dies, your dog will break your heart.

JAMES HERRIOT (1916–1995)

Sun on my face, the feel of spring round the corner, and nobody anywhere in sight except a dog, are still enough to fill me with utter happiness.

ELIZABETH VON ARNIM (1866–1941)

Dogs love plum cake and affection equally.

PAM BROWN, B. 1928

The great pleasure of a dog is that you may make a fool of yourself with him and not only will he not scold you, but he will make a fool of himself too.

SAMUEL BUTLER (1835–1902)

The great thing about living with a dog is that you can lock the kitchen when you've had enough of them. But you can't really do that with a man.

LINDA MANLEY-BIRD

Thoughtful dog lovers know that to love a dog is to know sorrow and loss as well as joy and companionship. They are parts of a whole.

JON KATZ

# Goldfish, turtles and hamsters are pets. Dogs are family.

MARK R. LEVIN

He is an affectionate, devoted and sometimes hilarious companion. He has made life worth living.

JENNI MURRAY

Dogs come into our lives to teach us about love and loyalty. They depart to teach us about loss. We try to replace them but never quite succeed. A new dog never replaces an old dog; it merely expands the heart.

ERICA JONG, B. 1942

From the moment I opened my
front door and bent down to touch
Greta's head and give her a kiss,
which she exuberantly returned
in Labrador fashion,
I felt a special bond with her.

SALLY ROSENTHAL

Brothers and sisters,
I bid you beware
Of giving your heart
to a dog to tear.

RUDYARD KIPLING (1865–1936)

I can honestly say that my life would not be complete without my beloved dogs. The most important reason is that they have taught me to recognize love.

CHRISTINE MIELE

Dogs never seem to hold grudges
against humans.

JEFFREY MASSON, B. 1941

# Dogs do not find anything "agreeable";

they are wild enthusiasts.

BEL MOONEY

The dog truly loves us, sometimes beyond expectation, beyond measure, beyond what we deserve, more indeed than we love ourselves. No dog will ever lie to us about love.

JEFFREY MASSON, B. 1941

On stubby legs he ran to meet me,
wagging his tail like crazy,
his eyes celebrating and
welcoming my return.

JUDY MCFADDEN

Cats can take great pleasure in our company, but I find it difficult to imagine that my cats would risk their lives to save mine. I can easily imagine my dogs doing this without hesitation.

JEFFREY MASSON,
B. 1941

All dogs rely on their human parents to care for them — to make sure they are well fed, properly treated, and enjoy their short lives. In return, we get pure love, loyalty and happiness.

MARK R. LEVIN

They come into our lives and bring us such joy and happiness. When we have a bad day at work, we walk through the front doors of our homes and they are there to greet us, tail wagging and butt shaking. All of a sudden that bad day doesn't mean anything.

LONG ISLAND PETER

Pets are the only creatures who give humans unconditional love. Your pet never yells at you, rejects you, tells you to go to hell or argues with you.

MARK R. LEVIN

Sometimes a dog is more than a pet.
It can be a joy in good times,
a comfort in bad, an
unquestioning friend always.

JOHN GROGAN

He's almost always wearing a big smile, and his long, furry tail is constantly wagging. Well, actually, when he's really happy, his tail moves in a circle much like a propeller.

MARK R. LEVIN

# Cats can tolerate us, whereas dogs adore us.

JEFFREY MASSON, B. 1941

He's my playmate at the park,
my camping buddy,
my cuddle partner.

ANNA LUPACCHINO

This dog would never be a mere pet. She would be more like a force, a way of life, a way of looking at things, a friend, an inspiration, an adventure. She brought us the most intense pleasure, along with the most intense agony.

PETER MARTIN

No other animal mourns for a lost human friend in the way that a dog does. You cannot impress your dog with beauty, wealth, possessions, power, or physical prowess. We might fall in love with somebody for any of these qualities. A dog does not fall in love, the dog merely loves.

JEFFREY MASSON, B. 1941

No matter how we treat them, what we do to them, how little attention we pay to them, they are eager to please us, eager to be with us.

JEFFREY MASSON, B. 1941

He had spent his life giving everyone around him love, affection, and happiness.

MARK R. LEVIN

I would often get down on the floor, hold either  Pepsi or Sprite's head in my hands, and put my nose up against their nose. I would tell them how beautiful they are, how much I love them, and kiss them on the nose. They would stare into my eyes and seem to know exactly what I was saying and feeling. And I knew they loved me, too.

MARK R. LEVIN

# Dogs are ready…to forgive anything we do to them.

JEFFREY MASSON, B.1941

Dogs have no guile....They don't profess to love your work and then attack it. They don't lick you then bite to draw blood. In a world of hypocrisy and betrayal, dogs are direct. They never lie.

ERICA JONG, B. 1942

Dogs are the best. And as you say, their entire existence is to give us love and pleasure. They are selfless.

MARK R. LEVIN

A puppy can often bring out the
puppy in an aged dog.

JEFFREY MASSON, B. 1941

He looked at me with the most soulful eyes and I felt his comfort when he was in my arms.

ANNA LUPACCHINO

What do they want in return for the happiness they bring us? Love, unconditional love. A head to be scratched, a tummy to be rubbed, a ball to be thrown or a place on the couch. Not too much to be asked from a loyal friend. A loyal family member.

LONG ISLAND
PETER

Your dog is your only philosopher.

PLATO (C. 427–348 B.C.)

It is strange how so miniature a creature can fill so large a space with his presence. His absolute trust calls forth absolute benevolence; and though, strictly speaking, he is a parasite, in truth we are as dependent upon him as he is on us.

THEODORE DALRYMPLE

Money will buy a pretty good dog but it won't buy the wag of his tail.

JOSH BILLINGS (1818–1885)

How small, how helpless, how utterly gormless a puppy is.

CHARLOTTE GRAY, B. 1937

At moments of grief, Arthur would put his head on my knee, or lie like a huge beanbag on my feet. He was also my unofficial personal trainer, forcing me to walk three times a day, every day, whatever the weather.

ESTHER RANTZEN, B. 1940

It is by muteness that a dog becomes for one so utterly beyond value… where words play no torturing tricks….Those are the moments that I think are precious to a dog; when, with his adoring soul coming through his eyes, he feels that you are really thinking of him.

JOHN GALSWORTHY
(1867–1933)

I hugged him to me, nestling into his soft, downy coat, then placing a kiss on top of his head. He snuggled in, and as I felt the love coming from this wee pup, I realized that here was someone who would let me love him back.

NILALA GARDENER

The dog chooses us, not because it is confused about our identity, not because dogs think we are the marvel of creation, but merely because dogs love us....Dogs love us not only because we feed them, or walk them, or groom them, or protect them, but because we are fun.

JEFFREY MASSON,
B. 1941

[Dogs]…give up their affections and their devotion recklessly and serve to show us in a tangible way something that transcends what we know of other imperfect loves in this workaday world of demands and disappointments. Their message is simple. They are here to remind us, "You are loved."

SHANE GALLOWAY

Dog love is powerful stuff.

JON KATZ

I seem to spend a great deal of time just staring at the dog, struck by how mysterious and beautiful she is to me and by how much my world has changed since she came along.

CAROLINE KNAPP

A dog has an uncanny ability of turning a lonely moment into one where there's a companion who never takes life too seriously for too long.

JENNI MURRAY

However much humans may do for a dog, there is always a bit of them which remains doggedly independent of any owner — shared or otherwise.

ELINOR GOODMAN

Happiness is a warm puppy.

CHARLES M. SCHULZ (1922–2000)

Nirvana must be very like
a replete puppy's sleep.
A rapture beyond dreams.

PAM BROWN, B. 1928

Our friendship defined us. These days I can't think of myself, or of life before or after him, without imagining him here forever, like an inscription carved into my heart.

STEVE DUNO

One looks at a sleeping puppy —
and forgives it everything.

PAM BROWN, B. 1928

If I was upset or blue, he'd dote on me, put his head in my lap and… throw a paw over my leg, or follow me around the house. When I'd bawled the night before, he'd stuck to me like glue. He'd even tried to distract me by bringing over a ball, then grabbing his leash and dropping it at my feet.

STEVE DUNO

# Dogs are fantastic stress relievers.

ALLEN & LINDA ANDERSON

"Go away, you bad, bad dog."
And so he would, crawling across the
carpet on his belly, ears down, abject.

PAM BROWN, B. 1928

He became the focal point of our existence. If he knew a walk was imminent, he would leap in pure bliss like a ballet dancer.

LEO MCKINSTRY,
FROM *DAILY MAIL*, FEBRUARY 18, 2003

Once a dog loves you, he loves you always, no matter what you do, no matter what happens, no matter how much time goes by.

JEFFREY MASSON, B. 1941

There is something consoling
about stroking a pet when you feel
frightened and alone.

CHRISTOPHER S. WREN

What dogs do — particularly a middle-aged, confident, contented dog — is offer perspective. They can cause you to look at something from another angle, to realize, in an instant, how lucky you are.

ROY MACGREGOR

One of the underrated pleasures of having a dog, as I'd come to appreciate, was the cover it gives you for talking freely and fluidly to yourself. Having another body around, especially one who reacts to the sound of your voice — and won't take you on about the content — was far more appealing and comforting than I'd expected.

STEVEN WINN

My dogs have taught me so much — patience, unconditional love, and, of course, compassion. Additionally, they always remind me of the secret to happiness….They rejoice at everything — being with the ones they love, the same landscape they've seen a hundred times, or catching some scent in the air. I am constantly learning from them.

RORY FREEDMAN

Dogs are our link to paradise. They don't know evil or jealousy or discontent. To sit with a dog on a hillside on a glorious afternoon is to be back in Eden, where doing nothing was not boring — it was peace.

MILAN KUNDERA, B. 1929

Dogs effortlessly exhibit an
ease of well-being that philosophers
and seekers have thirsted after
for eternity.

MARI GAYATRI STEIN

Whle I run my toes over his arched spine, I actually feel my tension easing and my bunched-up muscles relaxing. I imagine (as most dog owners invariably do) that he "understands" me, understands what I'm saying to him.

SHOBHA DÉ,
FROM *SPEEDPOST*

Life without our dogs would be very empty. They are affectionate, entertaining and give you the most wonderful greeting when you come home.

WILLIAM ROACHE

He is going to stick to you,
to comfort you, guard you, and give
his life for you, if need be.

You are his pal.

JEROME K. JEROME (1859–1927)

$T$ests have in fact shown that simply stroking your dog…helps to normalize blood pressure, and can also help to lower stress levels.

BILLY ROBERTS, FROM *THE HEALING PAW*

One rattle of the biscuit tin and you've got friends for life. They sit and stare with solemn eyes, and if you don't take the hint, you get barked at.

JANINE CHUBB, AGE 10

A dog is a chance to express yourself without the fear of seeming foolish, a chance to share emotions that others of our kind too often repel — tenderness, outright joy, love.

GAIL PETERSEN

There is nothing like the loyalty and love dogs have for their families. Nothing.

MARK R. LEVIN

Although [humans and dogs] have much in common, they also complement each other by doing, viewing, and experiencing life in vastly different ways. They make up for each other's abilities or inabilities to cope with and thrive on this planet. No wonder dogs and humans had to find each other.

ALLEN & LINDA ANDERSON

Your dog will love you no matter
what you have become.

BEL MOONEY

[My dogs have] filled such a
lonely hole in my life, my constant
companions, I can't imagine how I
would cope if I were to lose them.
They're funny, affectionate and full
of the kind of energy that tends
to diminish with age and illness.
They're a daily injection of
joie de vivre.

JENNI MURRAY

Choosing a puppy is a most
difficult task — it's impossible not to
fall in love with every one you see.

STUART & LINDA MACFARLANE

He toils not, neither does he spin, yet Solomon in all his glory never lay upon a door-mat all day long, sun-soaked and fly-fed and fat, while his master worked…to purchase an idle wag of the Solomonic tail, seasoned with a look of tolerant recognition.

AMBROSE BIERCE
(1842–C. 1914)

To buy a pup is to invest in love.

PAM BROWN, B. 1928